# Black Rhino

Louise and Richard Spilsbury

Heinemann
L I B R A R Y

**H** **www.heinemann.co.uk/library**
Visit our website to find out more information about Heinemann Library books.

To order:
☎ Phone 44 (0) 1865 888066
▤ Send a fax to 44 (0) 1865 314091
▢ Visit the Heinemann Bookshop at www.heinemann.co.uk/library to browse our catalogue and order online.

First published in Great Britain by Heinemann Library, Halley Court, Jordan Hill, Oxford OX2 8EJ, part of Harcourt Education.
Heinemann is a registered trademark of Harcourt Education Ltd.

Editorial: Kate Bellamy, Diyan Leake, Cassie Mayer, and Katie Shepherd
Design: Michelle Lisseter and Ron Kamen
Illustrations: Bridge Creative Services
Cartographer: Vickie Taylor at International Mapping
Picture research: Hannah Taylor and Fiona Orbell
Production: Duncan Gilbert

Origination: Chroma Graphics (Overseas) Pte. Ltd
Printed and bound in China by South China Printing Co. Ltd

The paper used to print this book comes from sustainable resources.

10 digit ISBN 0 431 11423 4 (hardback)
13 digit ISBN 978 0 431 11423 1
10 09 08 07 06
10 9 8 7 6 5 4 3 2 1

10 digit ISBN 0 431 11431 5 (paperback)
13 digit ISBN 978 0 431 11431 6
11 10 09 08 07
10 9 8 7 6 5 4 3 2 1

**British Library Cataloguing in Publication Data**
Spilsbury, Louise and Richard
Save the black rhino. – (Save our animals!)
599.6' 68
A full catalogue record for this book is available from the British Library.

**Acknowledgements**
The publishers would like to thank the following for permission to reproduce photographs: Ardea pp. **4** top (Y A Betrand), **5** top left (J Rajput); Corbis pp. **7** (J McDonald), **13** (FLPA T Whittaker), **17** (C Hellier), **19** (B Mays), **21** (K Ward), **23**, **24** (M Harvey), **25** (Reuters J Ngwenya); Digital Vision p. **5** middle; Ecoscene p. **9** (E Bent); FLPA pp. **12** (Minden Pictures/Frans Lanting), **28** (J Brandenburg); Getty Images p. **26–27** (T Graham); Naturepl.com pp. **4** bottom left (M Carwardine), **29** (P Oxford); Oxford Scientific pp. **4** middle, **5** top right, **10** (S Turner), **14** (Survival), **16** (Gallo Images), **22**; Panos Pictures p. **18** (S Thomas); Steve Bloom p. **6**; Still Pictures pp. **5** bottom, **11** (M Harvey), **15** (P Arnold/C&M Denis-Huot).

Cover photograph of black rhino reproduced with permission of Alamy Images/Alan Novelli.

The publishers would like to thank Nicky Springthorpe at Save the Rhino for her assistance in the preparation of this book.

Every effort has been made to contact copyright holders of any material reproduced in this book. Any omissions will be rectified in subsequent printings if notice is given to the publishers.

# Contents

Some words are shown in bold, **like this**. You can find out what they mean by looking in the Glossary.

# Animals in trouble

There are many different kinds, or **species**, of animal. Some species are in danger of becoming **extinct**. This means that all the animals from that species might die.

All the animals shown here are in danger of becoming extinct. These species need to be saved. The black rhino is one of them.

# The black rhino

Black rhinos are one of the biggest animals on Earth. An adult black rhino weighs as much as a car. They hide under bushes during the day.

*Black rhinos have very thick, wrinkly, tough, grey skin.*

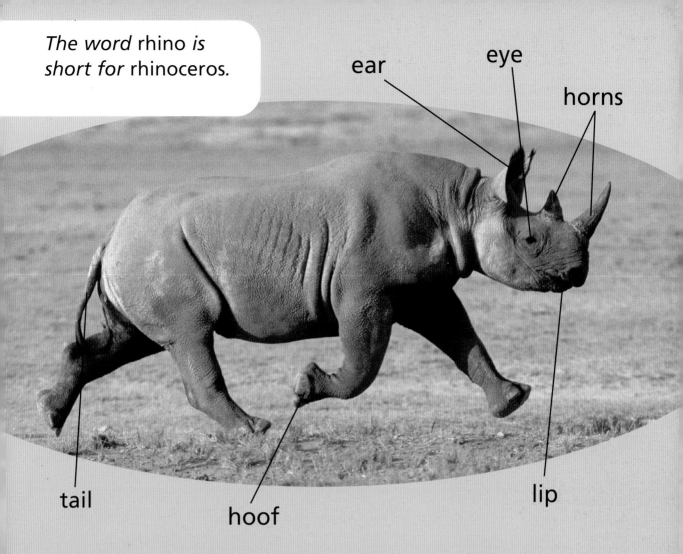

*The word* rhino *is short for* rhinoceros.

ear

eye

horns

tail

hoof

lip

A rhino has two horns on top of its head. It has big ears with hairy tufts, small eyes, and a pointed top lip. It has three hard toes called hooves on each foot.

7

# Where can you find black rhinos?

In the past, black rhinos lived in more than half of **Africa**. Today they only live in small areas of eastern and southern Africa.

This map shows where you might find black rhinos.

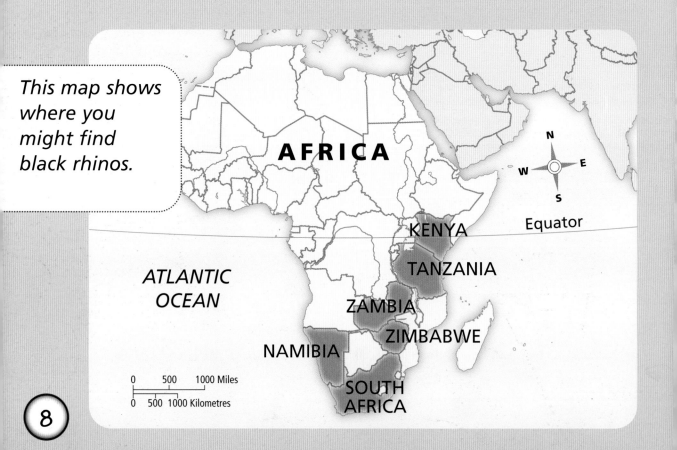

AFRICA

N
W • E
S

Equator

KENYA

TANZANIA

ATLANTIC OCEAN

ZAMBIA

ZIMBABWE

NAMIBIA

0   500   1000 Miles
0   500  1000 Kilometres

SOUTH AFRICA

The place where an animal lives is called its **habitat**. The black rhino's habitat is hot and dry with grasses, trees, and bushes.

*Rhinos do not come into the open when the sun is hot.*

# What do black rhinos eat?

Black rhinos are **herbivores**, which means they only eat plants. Black rhinos eat leaves, branches, and twigs from trees and bushes.

*A black rhino pulls leaves into its mouth like this.*

*This black rhino has been digging for food with its horn.*

Rhinos use their pointed top lip to break off bits of trees to eat. They use their big, flat teeth to chew their food.

# Young black rhinos

A baby black rhino is called a **calf**. The mother rhino usually hides her calf in the bushes or long grass to keep it safe.

*A black rhino calf can walk three hours after it is born.*

Rhinos are **mammals**. This means they feed on their mother's milk when they are very young. After two months the mother teaches her calf to find plants to eat.

*A black rhino calf stays with its mother for two years.*

# Natural dangers

Groups of lions or hyenas may kill a black rhino **calf** for food. Sometimes there are so many that a mother rhino cannot protect her baby.

*This black rhino mother is protecting her calf from hyenas.*

*Some other animals attack old, sick black rhinos.*

No animals attack a healthy adult black rhino. Rhinos are too big and strong. People are the biggest danger for black rhinos.

# Hunting for horns

Some people kill rhinos just to cut off their horns. These people are called **poachers**. They sell the rhino horns for a lot of money.

These people are helping a rhino that was caught by poachers.

Some people buy rhino horns to make knife handles. Most rhino horns are crushed and made into **traditional** medicines sold in some parts of **Asia**.

This expensive knife has a carved rhino horn handle.

# Dangers to the black rhino's world

The biggest danger to black rhinos comes from people. People cut down trees and build on the land. They take the water from ponds and rivers.

People are destroying the rhinos' **habitat**.

*Black rhinos need a lot of space and food.*

Now rhinos have less shade from the sun and fewer places to hide their **calves**. They also have to walk further to find enough water.

# How many black rhinos are there?

In 1970 there were about 65,000 black rhinos in **Africa**. Today there are only about 3,600. People need to help the rhino **population** grow again to save these animals.

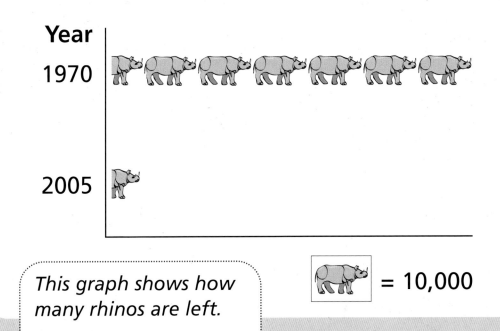

This graph shows how many rhinos are left.

= 10,000

Even if people help, it will take a long time before there are more black rhinos. A **female** only gives birth to one **calf** every three or four years.

*In some parts of Africa, black rhinos are rare.*

# How are black rhinos being saved?

Most countries have made laws to help protect black rhinos. Police follow and catch **poachers**. They stop people from buying or selling rhino horns.

The police have found all of these rhino horns.

*Wardens look out for poachers.*

Some countries have **reserves** where black rhinos are kept safe. Tourists pay to see them. Their money helps take care of the rhinos.

# Who is helping black rhinos?

Charities work to protect black rhinos. They tell people about the dangers rhinos face. They also raise money to pay for reserves.

This baby rhino's mother was killed by poachers.

Save the Rhino is a charity that helps black rhinos in eastern and southern Africa. It is bringing rhinos back to places where they had all been killed.

Charities are working to help rhinos live in the wild again in places where there are not many left.

# How can you help?

It is important to know that black rhinos are in danger. Then you can learn how to help save them. Read, watch, and find out all you can about black rhinos.

- Join a **charity** that raises money for black rhino projects. Try **WWF** or Save the Rhino.
- Visit zoos, **reserves**, or national parks where black rhinos live.

# The future for black rhinos

Black rhinos could be **extinct** by 2020. In some places **poachers** have killed nearly all the rhinos. In others, the rhinos' **habitat** is disappearing.

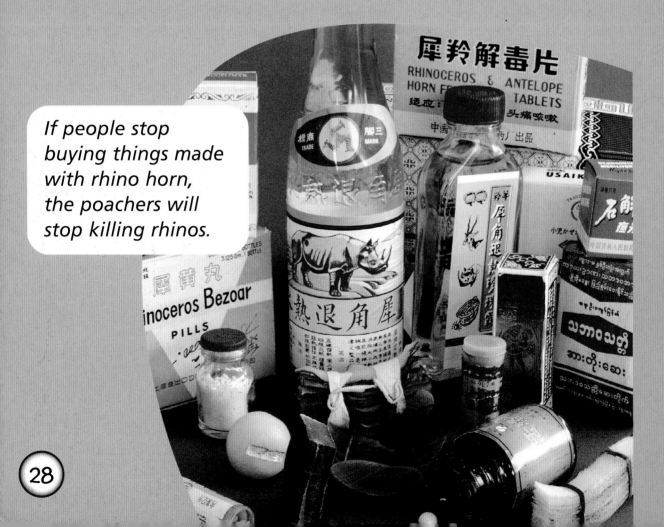

If people stop buying things made with rhino horn, the poachers will stop killing rhinos.

The good news is that in some areas, there are more black rhinos than there were a few years ago. People who live in these places want to help keep rhinos alive.

Tourists pay to see black rhinos. If there are no rhinos, they will not visit.

# Black rhino facts

- The word *rhinoceros* means "nose horn".
- Rhino horn is made of keratin, which is also found in human hair and nails.
- Black rhinos live for up to 35 years in the wild.
- Black rhinos are one of five **species** of rhino. Three live in **Asia** and two in **Africa**.
- Rhinos cannot see very well. They smell to find their way around.

# More books to read

*Black Rhino*, Malcolm Penny (Hodder Children's Books, 2001)

*Black Rhino*, Richard Spilsbury (Heinemann, 2004)

*Black Rhino*, Rod Theodorou (Heinemann Library, 2001)

# Websites

To find out more about **charities** that help rhinos, visit their websites:

Save the Rhino:  www.savetherhino.org

**WWF:**  www.wwf.org

# Glossary

**Africa**   a large continent. A continent is a large area of land divided into different countries.

**Asia**   the largest continent in the world

**calf**   baby rhino

**charity**   group that collects money to help animals or people in need

**extinct**   when all the animals in a species die out and the species no longer exists

**female**   animal that can become a mother when it grows up. Women and girls are female people.

**habitat**   place where plants and animals grow and live. A forest is a type of habitat.

**herbivore**   animal that eats only plants

**mammal**   animal that feeds its babies on the mother's milk and has some hair on its body

**poacher**   someone who hunts animals when it is against the law to do so

**population**   number of animals in a place

**reserve**   area of land where animals are protected

**species**   group of animals that are similar and can have young together

**traditional**   something that has been done the same way for many years

**WWF**   charity that used to be called the World Wildlife Fund

# Index